GAYLORD

SCIENCE **DISCOVERY** TIMELINES

KEY DISCOVERIES IN
ENGiNEERiNG
AND DESiGN

CHRISTINE **ZUCHORA-WALSKE**

LERNER PUBLICATIONS ◆ MINNEAPOLIS

FOR MY DAD, TONY WALSKE, THE CLEVEREST TINKERER I KNOW—AND FROM WHOM I INHERITED MY LOVE OF HISTORY AND SCIENCE

cover image
Engineer Richard Trevithick developed the steam train engine in the late eighteenth century. His invention led to steam-powered boats, farm equipment, and road vehicles, changing the face of transportation.

Content consultant: Gül Kremer, Professor of Engineering Design and Industrial Engineering, Penn State University

Copyright © 2015 by Lerner Publishing Group, Inc.

Lerner Publications Company
A division of Lerner Publishing Group, Inc.
241 First Avenue North
Minneapolis, MN 55401 USA

For reading levels and more information, look up this title at www.lernerbooks.com.

Main body text set in Diverda Serif Com. Typeface provided by Linotype AG.

Library of Congress Cataloging-in-Publication Data

Zuchora-Walske, Christine.
    Key discoveries in engineering and design / by Christine Zuchora-Walske.
       pages   cm — (Science discovery timelines)
    Includes bibliographical references and index.
    ISBN: 978-1-4677-5788-1 (lib. bdg. : alk. paper) — ISBN: 978-1-4677-6158-1 (pbk.)
  ISBN: 978-1-4677-6249-6 (EB pdf)
    1. Inventions—History—Juvenile literature. I. Title.
T48.Z83 2015
609—dc23   2014019899

Manufactured in the United States of America
1 — BP — 12/31/14

CONTENTS

INTRODUCTION

Engineering is using nature's energy and resources to help people. This field of study includes planning, designing, and constructing roads, bridges, dams, and buildings. It also includes inventing and improving machines, devices, materials, systems, and more.

Engineering has a long, fascinating history. That's because it's the story of people's efforts to fill needs, solve problems, and achieve goals. Perhaps people want to travel faster. They might need to overcome an obstacle, such as a river. They might want to share knowledge with one another or learn more about the universe. Engineered solutions to these problems include wheels, bridges, printing presses, and space shuttles.

Human efforts to design and build helpful tools often fail. But eventually, as people learn from these failures over time, engineering usually achieves its goals. When a goal is met, technology takes a leap forward. Suddenly people have a new tool for living or working. And society often changes in response to the new technology.

In ancient times, engineering focused on meeting basic survival needs. People needed to get food and water, to clothe and shelter themselves, and to protect themselves from animals. They developed tools and structures including weapons, wells, and wigwams to make survival a little easier.

Later on, the focus of engineering shifted to easing the labors of life. People developed new tools, such as wheels and plows, to help them carry loads and farm the earth. Tools like these increased the amount of daily work a person could accomplish.

Laborsaving tools freed up time for some people. These people were able to design and enjoy grand arenas, palaces, and places of worship. They could read and write, sharing ideas with the wider world.

In modern times, many people live in highly engineered environments. People live and work in buildings with electrical, plumbing, heating, cooling, security, and communications systems. They travel by bicycle, automobile, train, boat, and airplane. They communicate with phones, computers, and televisions. Just as engineering has affected the course of human history, it will continue to affect humankind's path to the future.

This Egyptian tomb painting from the 1200s BCE shows a servant plowing with oxen. Plows were one tool humans invented to make life easier.

A Line That Shows a Story

A timeline is a picture of history. It plots a series of events and their dates along a line. Timeline entries in this book tell the story of engineering. Entries on a timeline are always listed chronologically—in the order in which they happened.

A timeline helps people understand the cause-and-effect relationships between events. A timeline can span thousands of years or just a few minutes. Often pictures or photos illustrate the entries. Events that occurred before a certain point in history (in Christian tradition, the birth of Jesus Christ), include the abbreviation *BCE*, which means "Before the Common Era."

Each chapter in this book opens with a timeline, which is followed by the story of the events listed. Read the chapters in the way that helps you understand them best. You might read the stories first and then view the timeline entries. Or examine the timelines before checking out the intriguing stories behind them.

1

Before 4000 BCE

A variety of ancient civilizations build structures that contain primitive arches, such as slabs leaning together, lintels on posts, and corbeled arches.

300s BCE

The ancient Greeks learn about arches from the Egyptians, and true arches appear in a few Greek buildings. Ancient Roman builders adopt the true arch from the Greeks and use it for drains and city gates.

ca. 3000 BCE

People in ancient Mesopotamia and Egypt build arches of a completely different kind, called true arches.

THE **ARCH**

100s

Romans extend the concept of the arch to create roofs and ceilings called vaults and domes, which makes it possible to build large, spacious buildings.

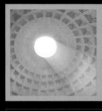

100s BCE

Roman architects develop and improve the arch so that it can cross wide spans and support a great deal of weight, making large bridges, aqueducts, and monuments possible.

700s

Muslim architects in modern-day Spain and Syria create variations on the Roman arch to add to their mosques.

Many thousands of years ago, people tasked with raising stone structures faced a problem. How could they make openings, such as windows and doorways, in their structures without weakening them? How could they create roofs and ceilings that would support their own weight and any weight above them? Openings were important for light, ventilation, movement, and defense. Roofs and ceilings, of course, provided shelter for people and objects housed in the space below. But windows or roofs with open space beneath them ran the risk of caving in.

Ancient humans may have found some ideas in nature to help them solve this problem. Maybe they saw two rocks or logs leaning against each other. Perhaps they spotted a boulder wedged high off the ground between two other rocks. No one can be sure what inspired the early structures those humans created.

PRIMITIVE **ARCHES**

People built primitive arches to meet the need for openings in their buildings. Primitive arches are not true arches, which are curved and came later, but primitive arches are arch*like*. They include triangular arches, posts and lintels, and corbeled arches. Archaeologists have found many examples of primitive arches among the remnants of ancient civilizations.

A triangular arch is a straight-sided opening formed by leaning two objects, such as bricks or slabs, against each other. In ancient Syria and Palestine, for example, builders used mud bricks to make triangular arches within the walls of ordinary buildings. These openings served as windows.

A post-and-lintel arch is a straight-sided opening as well—but it is rectangular instead of triangular. Two upright posts hold up a third piece, the lintel, laid horizontally across the tops of the posts. Post-and-lintel construction was very common in ancient Greece.

A corbeled arch is a bit like an upside-down staircase. To build a corbeled arch over an opening in a stone wall, the builder extends one end of a stone over each side of the opening and weights the other end of

This ancient Greek temple *(left)* used a post-and-lintel arch. The corbeled arch *(right)* can look like an upside-down staircase, with the stones coming together toward the top of the arch. The jagged edges of this corbeled arch were later smoothed out.

the stone. With each additional row of stones, the end pieces extending over the opening get closer. Eventually they meet in the center. Corbeled arches were common in ancient Egypt and Greece.

Primitive arches fulfilled the need for openings in stone structures. But all primitive arches shared one key disadvantage: they couldn't support very much weight. That meant that people couldn't make primitive arches very large. If they got too big, they collapsed. So primitive arches couldn't be used to make buildings with large doors or windows or large spaces inside them, unless columns were also used for support.

THE **TRUE ARCH**

Sometime around 3000 BCE, ancient people came up with a new kind of arch, commonly called the true arch. A true arch is made up of wedge-shaped blocks. When the wedges are placed together with their smaller ends aligned, they form a curve. A true arch is rounded, not triangular or rectangular like primitive arches.

Builders make a true arch by setting up a temporary wooden frame. Then they assemble the blocks, starting from the bottom of the arch. The top center stone, called the keystone, is the last block to be inserted. Then the builders remove the frame. When the frame is removed, the weight of the blocks presses them together.

A true arch is stronger than a primitive arch. When weight is added above the arch, its downward pressure forces the wedges together. In primitive arches, downward pressure forces the stones apart. A true arch is also able to span wider spaces than a primitive arch. That's because a large true arch is made of small, lightweight blocks, whereas a large primitive arch is made of huge stones that are hard to move and may collapse under their own weight.

HOW AN **ARCH WORKS**

An arch's wedge-shaped blocks are cut to fit together perfectly. These blocks are called voussoirs. Placed side by side, with their short and long ends aligned, the voussoirs form a curve from the central keystone (placed vertically at the top) down to the outermost footers (placed on their sides at the bottom).

The weight of the blocks puts pressure on the keystone. That makes the keystone push into the voussoirs around it. The pressure spreads sideways around the arch to the footers. Ultimately, the pressure goes partly down into the ground and partly out to the sides.

For an arch to work, it must always have strong material under it and to its sides. Strong structures called abutments at both ends of the arch prevent it from straightening out, spreading sideways, and collapsing inward.

This ancient stone doorway in Olympia, Greece, shows how the blocks of a true arch press together for stability.

No one knows who came up with the true arch. But the earliest known examples of it date from around 3000 BCE in ancient Mesopotamia (modern Iraq) and ancient Egypt. True arches appeared in ancient Greece in the 300s BCE. These early true arches were usually used for small structures, such as storerooms, tombs, sewers, and doorways—often concealed within a building or placed partially or fully underground. Most structures in these societies still used primitive arches.

Why didn't the Mesopotamians, Egyptians, and Greeks use the true arch more often? They likely knew the advantages. It's because they had several good reasons to stick with primitive arches. Handling smaller blocks of stone would have been easier for laborers, but Mesopotamian and Egyptian authorities weren't concerned about labor. They had plenty of servants.

True arch builders would have needed a lot more skill to cut and place the blocks properly and to build strong, stable foundations. Skilled

Ancient Egyptians used mud bricks to build this storehouse, probably during the thirteenth century BCE.

builders were in much shorter supply than unskilled workers. Wood too was scarce in Mesopotamia and Egypt. Greece had plenty of skilled workers and plenty of wood. But by the time the Greeks learned about true arches from the Egyptians, Greece already had firmly established building traditions people were reluctant to change.

ROMANS AND THE ARCH

Although the Greeks didn't use the arch much, it was important. Through the Greeks, their neighbors the ancient Romans learned about the true arch. In the 300s BCE, Roman builders began using the arch in small structures, such as drains and city gates.

Soon the Romans were using the arch in big structures too. They figured out how to stabilize large arches by building massive foundations beneath them or strong buttresses beside them. The Romans also strengthened arches by covering them with concrete—a strong, durable material made of lime and volcanic sand. The Romans built large arched bridges, aqueducts, theaters, monuments, and more. Some of these grand structures still stand.

PONT DU GARD

The Pont du Gard is a huge aqueduct the Romans built in the first century in southern France. It carried water across the Gardon River to supply the nearby city of Nemausus (modern Nimes). The Pont du Gard is still standing. It measures a whopping 1,181 feet (360 meters) long and 164 feet (50 m) tall. Each of its large arches measures 82 feet (25 m) wide.

As the Roman Empire grew stronger and larger, spreading all around the Mediterranean Sea through the 400s, the use of arches in building also spread. The Romans used the true arch so much it became known as the Roman arch. Roman builders even expanded on the concept of the arch. They created roofs and ceilings called vaults and domes. A vault is a series of arches lined up face-to-face. A dome is an arch rotated around its vertical axis. An early example of a dome is the Pantheon of Rome (in modern Italy), built in the early 100s. Vaults and domes opened up many new possibilities for large buildings.

Because of the Roman Empire's widespread use of the arch—and its relatives the vault and the dome—many cultures that came into contact with Rome also adopted the Roman arch. In this way, the Roman arch outlasted the Roman Empire, which began to collapse in the 400s. Throughout the Middle Ages (roughly 500 to 1500), Byzantine architects in eastern Europe and western Asia, as well as Romanesque architects in western Europe, used the round Roman arch constantly. Other cultures adapted the Roman arch and developed it further. In the Arab world, Muslim architects developed pointed, scalloped, S-curved, and horseshoe arches, which they used for mosques and palaces. The Great Mosque of

Damascus in modern Syria and the Great Mosque of Córdoba, in what is now Spain, have stood as examples of how Muslims embellished and enhanced the Roman arch during the eighth century. Arab and European explorers and traders eventually brought the arch concept to the rest of the world.

The Roman arch, vault, and dome have had long-lasting effects on human society. The ancient Romans made the first large structures in stone, brick, and concrete. Many of these structures still stand soundly in modern times. What is more, the Romans spread their ideas across a large portion of the world. Long after the fall of the Roman Empire, other cultures continued to copy Roman architecture. Roman building methods influenced the designs of structures around the globe, including the Hagia Sophia, a cathedral (later a mosque) in Istanbul, Turkey (500s); Chartres Cathedral in France (1100s); the Taj Mahal mausoleum in India (1600s); and the US Capitol in Washington, DC (1700s–1800s).

The Taj Mahal, one of India's most famous structures, includes Roman-style arches, vaults, and domes.

IRON **BRIDGES**

Engineers have continued to build arch bridges as well. Iron became available as a construction material for bridges in the 1700s. Using iron, engineers could adapt their arched bridge designs to better suit their situations. For example, a traditional arch bridge with the traffic deck on top of the arch isn't suitable for a wide river crossing in flat country. That's because the height of the arch needs to

The Gateshead Millennium Bridge in Newcastle, England, is a curved walkway with a curved steel arch above it for balance. The entire structure tilts sideways, raising the walkway into the air, to allow boats to pass underneath the bridge.

be half its span. In a flat area, the deck of a long traditional arch bridge would be so high above the land that a steep roadway would be needed to climb up to it. But using iron, engineers could build arch bridges with the deck below the top of the arch. The deck could be supported by the arch from above with iron rods, chains, or cables. Iron girders on the arch could support the deck from below. This kind of arch bridge is called a through arch because the roadway travels through the arch instead of over it.

The first iron bridge, a traditional arch bridge, was completed in 1779 across the River Severn in England. Iron bridges have remained popular in the centuries since. A particularly distinctive through arch bridge built over England's Tyne River opened to the public in 2001. The Gateshead Millennium Bridge is a through arch bridge with a curved deck. When boats need to pass under the bridge, the arch tilts downward, lifting the deck upward.

None of these structures would have been possible without the arch, the vault, and the dome. In addition, the arch, the vault, and the dome have made it possible to create countless smaller, more ordinary buildings, bridges, and other structures throughout the past two thousand years all around the world.

45,000 BCE
Ancient people around the world convey ideas by drawing, painting, and carving pictures.

140–86 BCE
In ancient China, people make the first true paper by beating plant fibers and forming the pulp into sheets.

3500 BCE
In ancient Sumer (modern southern Iraq), people start using pictographs—symbols that resemble the ideas they're meant to convey.

THE WORD

600s

In China, people begin using wood blocks to print books.

Early to mid 1800s

European and German American inventors develop a way to use iron instead of wood for building printing presses, as well as continuous rolls of paper and a steam-powered press. Printing becomes much faster and cheaper.

1450s

German businessman Johannes Gutenberg develops a printing press that uses movable metal type.

700s

The city of Samarqand (in modern Uzbekistan) shifts from Chinese to Arab control. Papermaking spreads to the Islamic world.

1200s

Through contact with Arab papermakers, Christian Europeans begin making paper in Italy.

The urge to physically record and share ideas has been a part of human nature for a very long time. Archaeologists have found evidence of this practice that goes back tens of thousands of years. Around 45,000 BCE, an early human in eastern Europe carved a picture on the tooth of a woolly mammoth. About 35,000 BCE, someone in southern Africa notched a bone, perhaps for counting. And around 30,000 BCE, people in western Europe painted animals on the walls of caves.

According to the evidence that scientists have found so far, carvings, pictures, and sculptures were humankind's main way of recording ideas for many years. It wasn't until the fourth millennium BCE that methods began to change.

In the ancient land of Sumer (modern southern Iraq), people kept track of their goods with small clay triangles, spheres, and cones. Historians believe these tokens represented different goods, such as sheep, measures of grain, and jars of oil. People stored the tokens in hollow clay balls and recorded the contents of each ball by pressing the tokens into the outside of the ball. Then they scratched pictographs, or simple pictures representing the tokens, into the clay. These pictures gradually evolved into symbols that carried meaning. People no longer needed to keep tokens as records, so they flattened the clay balls into tablets. Before long, Sumerians had developed the world's first written language to help them record and communicate ideas.

This Sumerian clay tablet dates back to around 2500 BCE. Pictographs such as these were one stage in the development of the world's first written language.

PAPER AND **EARLY PRINTING**

Over the next few millennia, people in many locations developed their own writing systems. Some people pressed symbols into soft clay. Others wrote with ink on silk or other fabric, bark or other plant surfaces, or animal skins. Still others carved or scratched symbols into wood, stone, or bone. Then, between 140 and 86 BCE, someone in ancient China made the first true paper by beating vegetable fibers and forming the pulp into sheets.

Several centuries later, in the 600s, the Chinese began printing books. They used carved wooden blocks to press ink onto paper. Not long after that, in the 700s, the Chinese-controlled city of Samarqand (in modern Uzbekistan) was conquered by Arabs. When this happened, knowledge of papermaking and block printing spread to other areas under Arab rule. From Samarqand, papermaking expanded to Baghdad (in modern Iraq) in the 700s and to Damascus (in modern Syria), Egypt, and Morocco by the 900s.

A few hundred years later, papermaking techniques made it to Europe. Through contact with Arab papermakers, people in Italy learned to make paper in the 1200s. A century later, Europeans produced their first block-printed items: playing cards.

The oldest printed book that still exists was made in China in the 800s. It includes pictures of Buddha and his disciples.

WHAT IS PAPER, ANYWAY?

True paper is a thin sheet made from fiber that has been soaked in liquid and beaten to a pulp, separating each individual thread. Using a screen, a person lifts the pulp from the water. As the pulp dries, it becomes a sheet of intertwined fiber on the screen. This sheet of matted fiber is paper.

By this definition, many things that people consider to be paper aren't paper at all. Parchment, for example, is a specially prepared animal hide—usually from a sheep or a goat. Papyrus *(right)* is made from a water plant with woody stems that are sliced and pasted together. Rice paper is a very thin layer of plant tissue from a small tree.

Until this time, books in Europe had been mostly Bibles and other religious texts. People made books entirely by hand. It took a lot of skill and time—usually many years—to make a book. That wasn't a problem because the demand for books was low. Most people couldn't read or write. Those who could were generally religious scholars, and they didn't share their books with the public.

Around the time paper and block printing came to Europe, European society was changing. A class of merchants arose. These people made their living buying and selling goods, instead of making things and growing food. Cities were growing. People were expanding their interests. They wanted to learn about the world as well as about religion. The first European university was founded around 1119, and others soon followed. They created a demand for books about all sorts of subjects.

THE FIRST **PRINTING PRESS**

Professional writers called scribes could not keep up with the demand for books. So Johannes Gutenberg, a German goldsmith and businessman, developed a tool to fill this need. He thought he could make lots of money on a device that could produce books quickly and cheaply. In the 1450s, Gutenberg developed a printing press by bringing other technologies together. He combined the use of paper with the ideas behind block printing and pressing grapes or olives to make wine or oil. Gutenberg himself supplied the final piece of the puzzle. He figured out an efficient way to make large amounts of movable metal type.

Here's how Gutenberg's press worked: First, the printer arranged metal letters in a frame called a chase to create a form, or backward image of the page to be printed. The printer attached the form, type facing down, to a screw that could be raised and lowered with a hand crank. The printer then applied ink to the form, used a movable plank to position paper under the form, and pressed the form onto the paper. This pressing movement was inspired by oil- and wine-making machines. The printer repeated this process to create as many copies of the page as were needed.

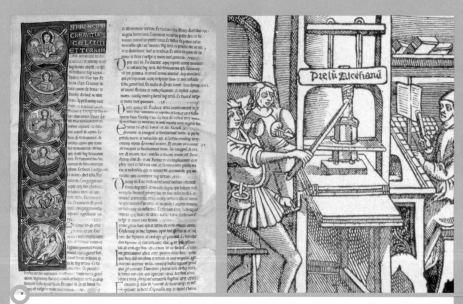

Some of the most popular printed pages in the twelfth century were religious texts *(left)*. In the 1400s, Johannes Gutenberg developed a printing press *(right)* using movable metal type and a pressing motion adapted from wine-making machines.

Printing caused far-reaching social changes. It helped spread new ideas in science, art, literature, philosophy, and politics. Many of these ideas helped bring about the Protestant Reformation, a sixteenth-century movement in which some people worked to change certain practices within the dominant religions of the time. Printing both fed and increased a hunger for education. The rise of an educated middle class chipped away at rigid social customs separating powerful noble families from powerless peasants. Books also changed the way people remembered and recorded history. Written records began to replace oral records.

IMPROVEMENTS TO **PRINT TECHNOLOGY**

Gutenberg's print technology didn't change much until the 1800s, when engineers made four important improvements. In 1800 British politician and scientist Charles Stanhope designed a printing press made completely of iron instead of mostly wood. The Stanhope press needed much less muscle power and could print bigger pages. In Germany, Friedrich Koenig was responsible for two improvements. In 1810 he patented a steam-powered printing press that used long rolls of paper instead of individual sheets. And in the United States, Ottmar Mergenthaler patented the first linotype machine in 1884. A typesetter used the linotype's keyboard to mechanically assemble a line of letter molds. These were then filled with molten metal. This created a single line, or slug, of type. Linotype slashed the time and the number of workers needed to create a page of type. Printing suddenly became far faster and cheaper. This helped mass media such as newspapers to flourish.

Later inventions continued to transform the printing process. These include the typewriter, the photocopier,

A plate from Charles Stanhope's 1800 iron printing press

FROM PRINT **TO DIGITAL**

Here's a glimpse of the way print and other media have changed in the United States: In 2014, 87 percent of American adults use the Internet. Fifty-three percent of these users believe that it would be very hard or impossible to give up the Internet. So digital information has become a normal part of American life. The vast majority of Americans get news in some digital format. In 2013, 82 percent of Americans said they got news on a desktop or a laptop, and 54 percent said they got news on a mobile device.

computer word processing, computer printing, and the Internet. Just as Gutenberg's printing press did in the 1400s, modern engineering is changing not only the ways in which people communicate but also how their communications affect one another.

These days, people can quickly and easily print text, images, and even three-dimensional (3-D) objects. In 1982 a technician at a Japanese research institute made the first model of a 3-D printer.

A 3-D printer can squeeze out plastic, metal, ceramics, food, or even plant or animal tissue. Using special computer software, a person can design any object on a computer and then load the design instructions into the 3-D printer. For a couple of hours, the printer nozzle zips back and forth, oozing out goo layer by layer until the desired object is complete.

Over the next few decades, 3-D printer technology improved and spread to different industries, including the automotive, aviation, and health-care industries. In 2011 doctors and engineers even used a 3-D printer to make a prosthetic jaw!

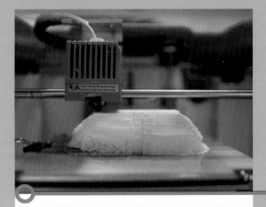

People use 3-D printers to make many different kinds of things. This 3-D printer is producing part of a robot.

Late first century
Greek mathematician Hero invents a steam-powered engine he calls the aeolipile.

1698
Englishman Thomas Savery uses the vacuum power of condensing steam to create a water pump.

1601–1606
Italian scholar Giovanni Battista della Porta suggests that steam condensed to water inside a closed chamber creates a vacuum.

1679
French scholar Denis Papin invents the first pressure cooker.

AHEAD

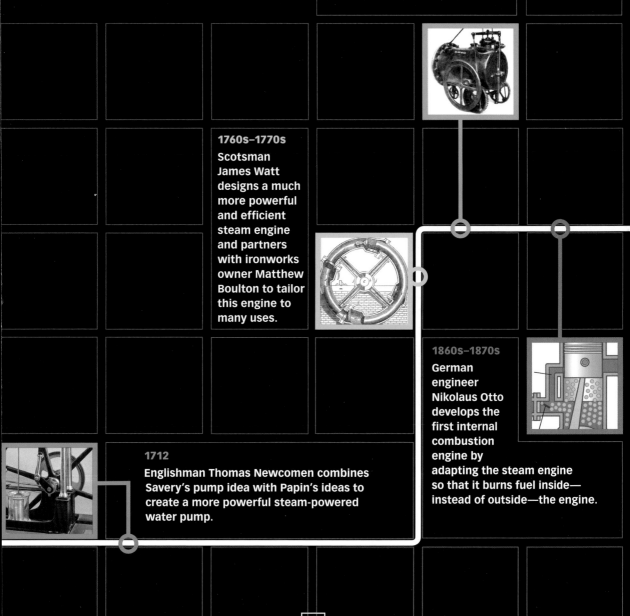

1797
Englishman Richard Trevithick develops a high-pressure steam engine, which makes steam-powered transportation possible.

1760s–1770s
Scotsman James Watt designs a much more powerful and efficient steam engine and partners with ironworks owner Matthew Boulton to tailor this engine to many uses.

1860s–1870s
German engineer Nikolaus Otto develops the first internal combustion engine by adapting the steam engine so that it burns fuel inside—instead of outside—the engine.

1712
Englishman Thomas Newcomen combines Savery's pump idea with Papin's ideas to create a more powerful steam-powered water pump.

Modern people know the steam engine as a machine that's handy for doing many different kinds of work. People generally know that it's been in use for a few centuries. What few realize, however, is that the idea was born about two thousand years ago as a toy.

HERO'S **AEOLIPILE**

The steam engine was first described by Hero, a Greek mathematician and engineer who lived in Alexandria, Egypt, in the first century. Hero called his device an *aeolipile*, which means "wind ball." Hero's aeolipile was made of metal. It consisted of a sealed cauldron of water over a fire. Two pipes led up out of the cauldron and into opposite points of a hollow ball. The ball could spin on the axis formed by the two pipes. Two more curved pipes with open ends stuck out of the ball. When heated to boiling, the water in the cauldron turned into steam, a gas. Gaseous water has a greater volume than liquid water, so steam escaped the cauldron into the ball. Then the steam escaped the ball through the open pipes. These pipes served as jets, making the ball spin.

There's no evidence that the ancient Greeks ever used their aeolipile for practical work. Later civilizations didn't either, as far as modern historians know, for about sixteen centuries.

The Greek mathematician Hero *(second from left)* developed the aeolipile *(center)*, which used steam to spin a ball. Later engineers used Hero's ideas in other steam-powered machines.

VÉRITABLE EXTRAIT DE VIANDE LIEBIG.

1. Historique de la machine à vapeur.
Expériences de Héron avec la vapeur, 120 ans avant J.-C.

But that doesn't mean humans had forgotten about the power of steam. Replicas of Hero's aeolipile were popular in the 1500s and the 1600s. In the early 1600s, Giovanni Battista della Porta, a scholar in Naples (in modern Italy), pondered the ideas behind the aeolipile. If water that changes to steam inside a closed container increases the pressure in the container, what would happen if the process was reversed? Della Porta suggested that steam condensing into water inside a closed chamber would *decrease* the pressure in the chamber and create a vacuum. This understanding of steam played a key role in future developments.

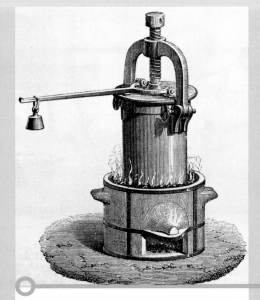

Denis Papin's steam digester was the first pressure cooker. Later scientists used principles of this device to invent the steam engine.

In 1679 French scientist Denis Papin invented a cooking device he called a steam digester. This closed container with a tight-fitting lid trapped steam to create high pressure inside the container. His invention was the first pressure cooker. Papin later noticed that the steam in his cooker tended to raise the lid. In 1690 this gave him the idea of using steam to drive a piston inside a closed cylinder full of water. When the water was heated, the expanding steam would push up the piston. When the steam cooled and became liquid water again, the vacuum would pull down the piston. Although Papin never built a steam engine of his own, other engineers picked up on his idea.

A NEW WATER PUMP

Around this time, England urgently needed fuel. Timber cutting for shipbuilding and firewood was eating up England's forests. The English had no good substitute for wood in shipbuilding, but they did have another potential power source: coal. Up until this time, the nation's coal mines were mostly on Earth's surface. Extracting more coal meant digging deeper mines. Deeper mines were more likely to fill with seeping groundwater. So the urgent need for coal created an urgent need for a new way to pump water out of coal mines. The old way, a series of buckets on a pulley system run by horses, was slow and expensive.

In 1698 English engineer Thomas Savery used the vacuum power of condensing steam to create a water pump. Savery's pump worked by boiling water to make steam, filling a tank with the steam, and cooling the tank to condense the steam and create a vacuum. That vacuum could pull water up from a mine. But Savery's pump was not very powerful. It could pump water only from a few yards deep. Also, the pump's boiler was not very strong. It often exploded from the high pressure of steam inside it.

In 1712 Englishman Thomas Newcomen combined Savery's pump idea with Papin's piston idea to create a more powerful steam-driven water pump. Newcomen's engine included a steam-filled cylinder cooled

Thomas Newcomen's steam-powered water pump could remove groundwater from coal mines. The pump combined elements of both Thomas Savery's water pump and Denis Papin's piston idea.

by a quick injection of cold water to create a vacuum. The vacuum pulled down a piston, which pulled down a chain. The chain in turn pulled down a seesawing beam, which lifted a pump attached to the other end of the beam. A weight on the pump end of the beam lowered the pump as the water turned to steam again.

Coal mines used Newcomen's engine for almost sixty years. It was a big improvement over previous methods. But it still wasted a lot of heat, fuel, and time. The water had to be heated and cooled for each cycle.

James Watt worked on scientific and mathematical instruments at the University of Glasgow, Scotland. In the 1760s, he was asked to repair the university's Newcomen engine. He did so and learned how wasteful the engine was. So Watt designed a new, more efficient, much more powerful steam engine. Watt's engine had separate chambers for heating water and cooling steam.

HOW A **ROTARY STEAM ENGINE** WORKS

A steam engine has the following six basic parts:

1. An external heat source
2. A boiler full of water
3. A valve
4. A cylinder
5. A piston
6. A wheel

The heat source, such as a coal fire, heats the water inside the boiler. When the water gets hot enough, it becomes steam, and its volume grows sixteen hundred times bigger. The expanding steam presses against the inside of the boiler and escapes with great force through the valve into the cylinder. Inside the cylinder, the moving steam pushes the piston back and forth. A crank connects the piston's rod to a wheel, which converts the piston's back-and-forth movement into rotary, or rotating, motion.

RICHARD TREVITHICK:
SLOW OR BRILLIANT?

Richard Trevithick had lots of trouble in school. His teachers thought he was lazy, and he never really learned to read or write. But Trevithick was very skilled with machinery. Even his engineering successes were criticized, though. James Watt himself thought Trevithick's high-pressure engine was a terrible idea. The engine was definitely dangerous at first. It worked, but it tended to explode after a few uses. The engine was gradually improved, and these days, Trevithick is considered one of the most important inventors of his time.

Watt partnered with ironworks owner Matthew Boulton in the 1770s to begin producing Watt steam engines. Together, they improved the engine so that it could spin a wheel. This rotary motion meant that Watt's steam engine could be used to power many kinds of machines as well as to pump water. The improvements helped steam technology spread quickly.

The steam engine made steamboat travel and commerce possible. The earliest steamboats could go as fast as 8 miles (13 kilometers) per hour downstream or 3 miles (4.8 km) per hour upstream.

POWERING MANY KINDS OF MACHINES

Watt's engine set the stage for the Industrial Revolution, a combination of major changes in farming, manufacturing, mining, and transportation. That's because Watt's engine made mining easier. Easier mining meant plentiful coal. Plentiful coal meant that Watt's engine could power machines of many kinds, including factory, mining, and farm equipment.

When Englishman Richard Trevithick developed a smaller, high-pressure engine in 1797, the steam engine became more powerful than ever. Steam-driven transportation became possible. Throughout the 1800s, steam engines were added to boats, trains, farm vehicles, and road vehicles.

The steam engine burned coal, because no other widely available fuel provided as much energy. People eventually used coal for heating and powering electrical generators too.

HOW A **STEAM TURBINE** GENERATES ELECTRICITY

A turbine has three main parts: a rotor, a shaft, and a generator. The rotor looks like a fan or a pinwheel with many blades. The blades are attached to a central piece called a hub. As steam pushes on the blades, they move. This motion makes the hub spin. (Alternatively, an engine can spin the rotor.) The hub is attached to the rod-shaped shaft. As the hub spins, it spins the shaft. The spinning shaft is attached to an electric generator. The generator contains strong magnets and coils of wire. As the shaft spins the magnets, they push electrons through the wire. The flowing electrons create an electric current inside the wire.

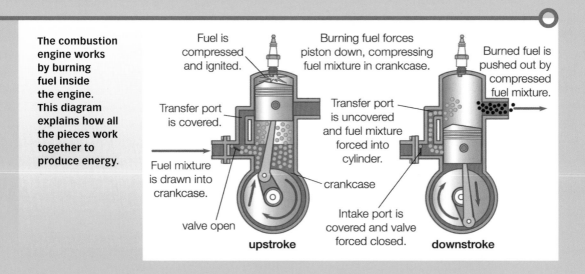

The combustion engine works by burning fuel inside the engine. This diagram explains how all the pieces work together to produce energy.

Fuel is compressed and ignited.

Transfer port is covered.

Fuel mixture is drawn into crankcase.

valve open

upstroke

Burning fuel forces piston down, compressing fuel mixture in crankcase.

Transfer port is uncovered and fuel mixture forced into cylinder.

crankcase

Intake port is covered and valve forced closed.

Burned fuel is pushed out by compressed fuel mixture.

downstroke

For about two centuries, coal was the king of fuels. But it wasn't perfect. This technology required coal miners to extract the coal from underground mines. This was very hard—and sometimes very dangerous—work. Burning coal also produced air pollution, which often leads to illness in people.

In the 1860s, German engineer Nikolaus Otto, along with other inventors in Belgium and France, began experimenting with the internal combustion engine (ICE). These engines work by burning fuel inside the engine, instead of in a separate chamber. Fuel burns inside cylinders in the ICE. This releases energy that makes pistons move, and those moving pistons can turn a vehicle's wheels.

Over the following decades, inventors found that gasoline, which is made from oil, was the ICE's perfect fuel and that the ICE was an ideal engine for the automobile. Henry Ford started the first moving assembly lines in the early 1900s, producing automobiles that ordinary people could buy. By the late 1920s, millions of automobiles had rolled off assembly lines. Businessmen started huge oil companies to provide gasoline for all these vehicles. Within a few decades, oil became a crucial resource. Steam continued to be used in mining, agriculture, and oil drilling, but gas eventually replaced it as the most used fuel source, partly because people believed oil was so abundant and partly because engineers learned how much more efficient gas-fueled engines could be.

In the twenty-first century, industrialized nations still rely heavily on fossil fuels such as coal, oil, and natural gas. Factories and power plants are the main users of coal and natural gas. Oil is the world's primary transportation fuel. Steam engines are no longer common except in power plants that generate electricity. But the fact remains that many, if not most, modern machines have some historical connection to Watt's steam engine.

Steam is not necessarily just a fuel of the past, either. In some corners of the engineering world, people are trying to revive steam power by addressing the drawbacks that led to steam's demise in the early 1900s—reducing the steam engine's pollution and increasing its efficiency. For example, in the early 2000s, a team called the British Steam Car Challenge (BSCC) began designing a modern steam-powered automobile. In 2009, after many failed attempts, BSCC finally broke the land-speed record set by the Stanley Steamer automobile in 1906, just before ICE vehicles overtook steam-powered autos. The BSCC vehicle, named *Inspiration*, achieved a speed of 139.843 miles (225 km) per hour—nearly 13 miles (21 km) per hour faster than the Stanley Steamer ever went. The BSCC team hopes that its achievements will inspire other engineers to revive steam power for modern uses.

Charles Burnett III, who drove and financed the *Inspiration*, stands next to the steam-powered car after breaking the land-speed record in 2009.

4 COUNTING BOARDS

300 BCE
The ancient Babylonians use the first counting boards.

1623
German scholar Wilhelm Schickard designs a machine called a calculating clock, the first known mechanical computer.

1820s–1830s
Englishman Charles Babbage designs the difference engine and the analytical engine, two types of steam-powered mechanical calculators.

ca. 1200
The Chinese, the Maya, and the Aztecs each develop a form of the abacus.

1939

Americans John Atanasoff and Clifford Berry build the first all-electronic computer using vacuum tubes.

1958

Americans Jack Kilby and Robert Noyce invent the integrated circuit, which combines the functions of the transistor and other parts in computers.

Late 1880s

American Herman Hollerith builds the first electromechanical punch-card data processing machine for use in the 1890 US census.

1971

The Intel company releases the first microprocessor, dramatically lowering the cost and complexity of making computers.

Just as it's hard to imagine life without the written word, it's also hard to imagine life without written numbers. But tens of thousands of years ago, neither of these tools existed. Back then, people simply counted with their fingers and toes. If they needed to count larger quantities, they used other items, such as rocks or sticks, as makeshift counters.

Such counters weren't exactly convenient. If a person needed to move about and count objects, the counters needed to be toted along. If a quantity was very large, it wasn't practical to use individual counters. To address these problems, eventually people began using counting devices instead of rocks, sticks, and other individual counters.

COUNTING BOARDS **AND THE ABACUS**

The earliest counting devices were counting boards. The ancient Babylonians, who lived in Mesopotamia, were probably the first to use these, sometime around 300 BCE. The simplest counting boards used pebbles on the ground. A person drew lines in the dirt and placed pebbles between those lines to represent amounts. For example, the space between the first two lines might represent the ones place, and each marker in that space represented one unit. The space between the second and third line might represent the tens place, and each marker in that space represented ten units. Fancier counting boards were made of grooved wood, clay, stone, or metal tablets with pebbles, marbles, or disks for markers.

Counting boards were an improvement over individual counters, but the markers were easy to lose. The ancient Roman civilization solved this problem by using slots instead of grooves. The slots contained sliding beads that could not fall out. This idea spread outward from the Roman Empire, eventually reaching China, where it evolved into the abacus around the year 1200. An abacus is a frame that holds rods with sliding beads on them. The Maya and Aztec civilizations of Central America also developed their own forms of the abacus around this time.

A skilled user could make very fast calculations on an abacus. But it was not a calculator or a computer. It didn't do any math automatically. It required human intelligence to make calculations.

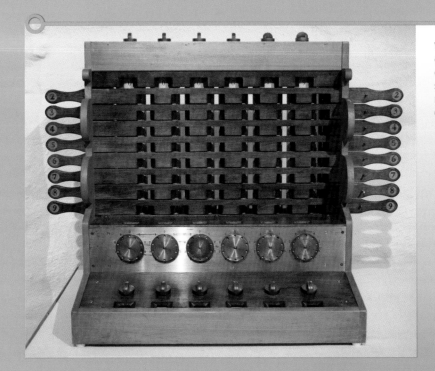

Wilhelm Schickard's calculating clock could add, subtract, and multiply up to six-digit numbers.

EARLY **CALCULATORS**

The first known computer, a mechanical calculating machine, came along several centuries later. In 1623 German scholar Wilhelm Schickard designed a machine he called a calculating clock. It used gears and wheels to add, subtract, and multiply. A complete revolution of the ones wheel moved the tens wheel a single increment and so on, in much the same way a car odometer works. The calculating clock could handle up to six digits. It warned the user by ringing a bell when it had reached its calculating limit.

After Schickard, many other scholars devised different kinds of mechanical calculators. A couple of centuries passed before someone came up with a fully automated calculator. That person was Englishman Charles Babbage.

In the early 1820s, Babbage realized that long calculations are often made up of many similar, repeated operations. The steam engine had been invented by this time, and people were using it widely to do repetitive tasks in mining and manufacturing. Babbage thought the steam engine could work for mathematics too. So he designed a machine he called a difference engine. It was a huge steam-powered mechanical calculator designed to print astronomical tables—charts that help scientists predict the positions

Charles Babbage's difference engine was a steam-powered calculator designed to be used in astronomy.

of the sun, the moon, planets, and stars. Babbage started building the difference engine, but another idea sidetracked him. He called the new idea an analytical engine. It would be a mechanical computer that could solve any math problem. It would use paper cards with holes punched in them to represent numbers and trigger operations. It would produce answers on punch cards as well.

Over several decades, Babbage eventually built a difference engine. It was gigantic—about the length of a small car—and very expensive. A few other people built similar machines, but they were so big and costly that the difference engine never became widely used.

COUNTING THE CENSUS

Babbage's analytical engine stayed on the academic back burner until the 1880s, when an urgent need in the United States sparked renewed interest in the idea. The 1880 US census, for which employees had done all the math by hand, had taken seven years to complete. The population was growing quickly, and officials feared that the 1890 census would take even longer. In fact, they feared they wouldn't finish before it was time for the next census in 1900. So they held a competition to find a better method. A census office employee, Herman Hollerith, won the competition. Hollerith borrowed Babbage's analytical engine concept and built the first electromechanical punch-card data processing machine.

Here's how Hollerith's tabulating machine worked. First, a worker put a thick piece of paper in the device. The machine punched holes in certain places on the paper. The punches represented information from the census. Then a worker put the paper into a different part of the machine that could interpret the punched information. Underneath the paper were pools of the element mercury. Metal pins went through the holes and touched the mercury, which made an electric circuit. The completed circuit moved a counter forward and signaled a worker that those punches had been counted.

The 1890 census used Hollerith's machine, which produced final results in a mere six weeks. After this grand success, Hollerith started his own business to make and market similar machines. He called it the Tabulating Machine Company. A few decades later, it became International Business Machines (IBM).

The Hollerith tabulator was a big step in computing. But like Babbage's difference engine, it was a bulky machine with lots of moving parts. By the 1900s, electricity was widely used and engineers wanted to create a completely electronic computer. Without the need for hundreds of gears and shafts to represent numbers and their possible relationships,

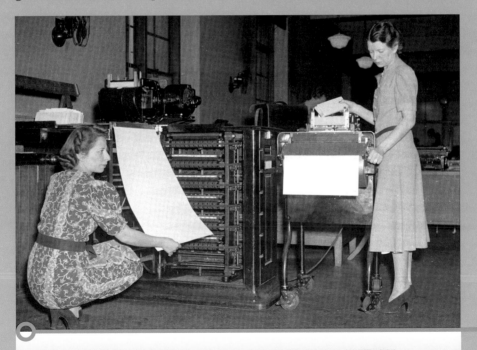

A US census worker *(left)* shows a punch card used in Herman Hollerith's tabulating machine *(center)*.

WHAT EXACTLY IS A **COMPUTER?**

A computer is a machine that can be told, or programmed, to do certain things. It holds and processes information called data. Hardware and software are the two main kinds of parts that make up a computer. Hardware is made up of the visible, tangible pieces, such as the screen or the keyboard. Software, or programs, are the components that tell a computer what to do.

Input is information a user puts into a computer. When a person puts information into a computer, the computer processes that input and produces new information called output. Input and output may include words, numbers, sound, pictures, or video.

an electronic computer could work much faster and could handle more complicated mathematics. In 1939 Iowa State College professor John Atanasoff and his student Clifford Berry built an all-electronic computer using the idea that any math equation can be stated simply as either true or false. They applied this idea to electronic circuits switched on or off inside vacuum tubes.

TRANSISTORS AND **INTEGRATED CIRCUITS**

Vacuum tubes had their own drawbacks, though. They used a lot of electricity and gave off a lot of heat. And when they got too hot, they often stopped working. To solve this problem, scientists at Bell Laboratories invented the transistor in 1947. A transistor is a tiny, solid electronic switch. It is sturdier, smaller, and more reliable than a vacuum tube. It also uses a lot less electricity. So a computer built with transistors is also smaller, faster, and more efficient than one built with vacuum tubes.

After the invention of transistors, the largest part of an electronic circuit was the awkward wiring among its parts. Transistors were small, but they had to be big enough to connect to all the other parts of the circuit. And all those pieces need to be there for the circuit to work. In Texas in 1958, Jack Kilby wondered if the whole circuit could be made in one piece, from the same material. Meanwhile, in California, Robert Noyce

Microprocessors *(left)*, developed in the 1970s, made it possible for computers to be much smaller than the first all-electronic computer *(below)* John Atanasoff and Clifford Berry built in 1939.

was working on a similar idea. Each experimenter used tiny threads of metal to connect the transistor and other electronic parts. They attached the metal threads to the other pieces. This created what's called an integrated circuit (IC). Thousands of transistors can fit onto an IC the size of a pencil eraser. Noyce got the first patent for the IC, but both men are remembered for developing the invention.

The invention of the IC ushered in the modern era of computers. Computers became stronger, lighter, and more dependable. Eventually, developers gave computers the ability to do more than one thing at once.

In 1971 the Intel company released the first microprocessor, a specialized IC. Tasks that had once needed many computer chips with connecting wires for arithmetic, logic, and control could now be done by one chip. This development lowered the cost and complexity of manufacturing computers. Before long, nearly every electronic device contained a microprocessor. Computers became common workplace and personal tools, growing smaller and smaller every year. Modern computers can do a lot more than math. They can receive, edit, display, and produce text, music, pictures, videos, and more.

These days, scientists are developing the next generation of computers: quantum computers. In a traditional computer, information is stored as bits that represent a value of either one or zero. A quantum computer

In 1947 John W. Mauchly and J. Presper Eckert Jr. at the University of Pennsylvania developed the giant Electrical Numerical Integrator and Calculator (ENIAC) machine *(right)*, an early vacuum-tube computer. It used eighteen thousand vacuum tubes, required punch-card input, weighed 30 tons (27 metric tons), and took up a 30- by 50-foot (9 by 15 m) space.

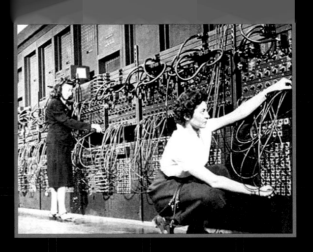

In 2014 scientists made an extremely tiny computer called a nanoelectronic finite-state machine (nanoFSM). It's only 0.01 by 0.001 inches (0.3 by 0.03 millimeters)! The nanoFSM's designers were able to fit hundreds of minuscule transistors into a very small package. The nanoFSM might someday be used in tiny medical devices or very small robots.

has quantum bits. So the individual particles in these bits can represent zero, one, or a value between them. A traditional computer calculates numbers by testing all the options of zeros and ones, one at a time. A quantum computer could test more options at once, which would speed up its calculations. A quantum computer will be fantastic at crunching numbers, which can help in cracking codes and searching databases. A Canadian company called D-Wave claims to have built the first quantum computer, but in 2014, scientists were still testing its capabilities.

AN ONGOING **STORY**

The developments of the arch, the printing press, the steam engine, and the computer make up just four of countless chapters in the engineering story. But these chapters demonstrate some important truths about all engineering—truths that apply no matter what problems people are trying to solve.

First, engineers must understand math and science, then use them creatively and persistently to solve problems. As people tried to harness the power of steam, for instance, they had to first understand the basic scientific principles of steam, such as increasing and decreasing pressure. Then they had to figure out how to use those ideas to develop steam technology. And understanding alone wasn't enough. They also had to work hard and persevere through failures before they achieved success.

Second, it usually takes a team to solve a complex engineering problem. Gutenberg could not have developed a successful printing press if others had not already invented paper, ink, and screw presses for crushing fruit. Nor can one person—no matter how clever—complete a large construction project, such as an aqueduct or a cathedral. Such projects need huge amounts of material and labor. Those resources come from governments, churches, businesses, and other organizations in the larger community.

Third, when people take a step forward in engineering, they make the next step possible. So each new tool provides a bridge to an even better tool. The development of the printing press led to the quick spread of scientific knowledge. That contributed to the development of the steam engine. The steam engine then made it possible to automate the printing press.

Finally, engineering achievements can have unintended consequences. While scientists and engineers try to consider all possible outcomes of a new technology, sometimes technology changes the world in unexpected ways. A new technology can solve a problem and also lead to a new problem. The development of the steam engine made coal mining easier. Easier mining meant plentiful coal, which people burned for heat and fuel. But this useful new achievement also filled the skies with soot and created the new problem of air pollution.

As time marches on, human society both influences and is influenced by engineering. Each generation inherits the technologies of its ancestors. Meanwhile, each generation faces a new set of needs, problems, and desires to address through engineering. The story of engineering is far from over. It is as old as humankind, and it will go on as long as humans do.

YOUR TURN ON THE TIMELINE

Milestones in engineering and design are much more than a list of dates. Use what you have learned in this book—as well as your imagination and creative writing skills—to compose a short story.

First, pick one of the events listed on the timelines at the beginning of each chapter. Next, imagine what it was like to live during that period in history. Choose a person who was involved in the breakthrough or make up a character who was affected by it. Then write a story about the engineering breakthrough you have chosen. Your story should show how this new technology affects a character's life. Remember to include sensory details, so your audience will feel as though they witnessed the event too.

After you finish writing, visit your local library or hop online. Try to find historical fiction related to the engineering milestone you selected. How do those tales compare with *your* story?

LERNER

Expand learning beyond the printed book. Download free, complementary educational resources for this book from our website, www.lerneresource.com.

SOURCE

GLOSSARY

abutment: something against which another thing rests its weight or pushes with force

axis: an imaginary straight line that an object spins around

buttress: a structure built against a wall or building to give support and strength

circuit: the complete path of an electric current

efficient: producing desired results without wasting time, energy, or material

mass media: methods of communication, such as newspapers, radio, or television, that are designed to reach many people

millennium: a period of one thousand years

odometer: an instrument for measuring distance traveled

patent: to get a legal document that gives an inventor the sole rights to make or sell an invention

piston: a sliding piece moved by the pressure of a fluid that usually consists of a short solid cylinder moving within a larger hollow cylinder

primitive: ancient or early

technology: a machine, piece of equipment, or method designed by humans

transistor: an electronic device that controls the flow of electricity in electronic equipment

type: a rectangular block, usually of metal, with a raised letter, number, or symbol from which an inked print is made

vacuum tube: a tube filled with almost no matter that is capable of containing a freely flowing electric current

valve: a movable part used to control the flow of liquid or gas

SELECTED BIBLIOGRAPHY

Cringely, Robert X. *PBS: Triumph of the Nerds*. PBS. 1996. https://www.pbs.org/nerds.

Hourihane, Colum. *The Grove Encyclopedia of Medieval Art and Architecture*. Vol. 1. New York: Oxford University Press, 2012. http://books.google.com/books?id=FtlMAgAAQBAJ&printsec=frontcover#v=onepage&q&f=false.

Lamb, Robert. "How Steam Technology Works." *How Stuff Works*. February 27, 2008. http://science.howstuffworks.com/steam-technology1.htm.

Lira, Carl. "Brief History of the Steam Engine." *Introductory Chemical Engineering Thermodynamics* supplement. Michigan State University. May 21, 2013. http://www.egr.msu.edu/~lira/supp/steam/.

University of Minnesota Media History Project. University of Minnesota. May 21, 2012. http://www.mediahistory.umn.edu.

FURTHER INFORMATION

ASCEville
http://www.asceville.org/
Try out the fun challenge of engineering with the help of the American Society of Civil Engineers' extensive gallery of interactive and hands-on civil engineering activities.

Cleveland, Donald. *Seven Wonders of Communication*. Minneapolis: Twenty-First Century Books, 2010.
Explore the first oral language, hieroglyphs and the development of written communication, telephones and cell phones, the World Wide Web, and robot communication.

Doeden, Matt. *Steve Jobs: Technology Innovator and Apple Genius*. Minneapolis: Lerner Publications, 2012.
This biography tells the story of a man who used his innovation and vision to help advance computer technology like no other.

NASA for Kids: Intro to Engineering
http://education.nationalgeographic.com/education/media/nasa-kids-intro-engineering/?ar_a=1
Learn about the basics of engineering and find many fascinating videos, articles, and links to help you learn more about real-life engineers.

O'Neill, Terence, and Josh Williams. *3D Printing*. Ann Arbor: Cherry Lake, 2014.
Learn how 3-D printers work and how to use them to bring your own designs to life.

Physics of Stone Arches
http://www.pbs.org/wgbh/nova/physics/arch-physics.html
See if you can build a cathedral arch without it collapsing, and learn more about the forces at work in this kind of architecture.

Samuels, Charlie. *The Rise of Industry (1700–1800)*. New York: Gareth Stevens Publishing, 2011.
The book explores the innovations of the 1700s that led to and made up the Industrial Revolution.

INDEX

PHOTO ACKNOWLEDGMENTS

The images in this book are used with the permission of: © Stock Connection Blue/Alamy, p. 5; © Raphael Van Butsele/Photographer's Choice/Getty Images, pp. 6 (top), 9 (left); © Tony Moran/Alamy, pp. 6 (middle), 11; © Samuel Magal, Sites & Photos Ltd./Bridgeman Images, p. 6 (bottom); © nobleIMAGES/Alamy, pp. 7 (top left), 13; © funkyfood London - Paul Williams / Alamy, p. 7 (bottom left); © ADB Travel/Alamy, p. 7 (right); © age fotostock Spain, S.L. / Alamy, p. 9 (right); © Prisma Archivo/Alamy, p. 12; © David Pearson/Alamy, p. 14; © Washington Imaging/Alamy, p. 15; © Bridgeman Images, p. 16 (top left); © Elitsa Lambova/Alamy, p. 16 (middle), 18; © Sovfoto/Universal Images Group/Getty Images, p. 16 (top right); © Werner Forman/Universal Images Group/Getty Images, pp. 17 (top left), 19; © Christie's Images/Bridgeman Images, p. 17 (middle left); © Bibliotheque Municipale de Bourges/Bridgeman Images, pp. 17 (bottom middle), 21 (left); © Ken Welsh/Bridgeman Images, pp. 17 (right middle), 21 (right); © Cliff Hide Local/Alamy, pp. 17 (top right), 22; © Archives Charmet/Bridgeman Images, p. 20; REUTERS/Ina Fassbender/Newscom, p. 23; © Look and Learn/Bridgeman Images, pp. 24 (top), 26; © Universal History Archive/UIG/Bridgeman Images, p. 24 (bottom left); © Oldtime/Alamy, p. 24 (bottom right); © Science, Industry and Business Library/New York Public Library/Science Source, pp. 24 (right) 25 and top middle); © Conservatoire National des Arts et Metiers, Paris/Giraudon/Bridgeman Images, pp. 25 (bottom middle), 28; © Science Source, p. 25 (top right); © Universal Images group Limited/Alamy, pp. 25 (bottom left), 32; © Oldtime/Alamy, p. 27; © Photo Researchers/Science Source, pp. 30, 35 (bottom left), 39; © Hywit Dimyadi/Dreamstime .com, p. 31; AP Photo/Chris Ison/PA Wire, p. 33; © Creditakg-images/John Hios/Newscom, p. 34 (top left); © Ekely/E+/Getty Images, p. 34 (bottom left); Herbert Klaeren/Wikimedia Commons (cc.3.0), p. 34 (top right); © Adam Hart-Davis/Science Source, p. 34 (bottom right); Manop/Wikimedia Commons (cc 3.0), pp. 35 (top middle), 41 (bottom); © Fox Photos/Getty Images, p. 35 (top right); © SSPL/Science Museum/Getty Images, pp. 35 (bottom right), 41 (top); Herbert Klaeren/Wikimedia Commons (cc.3.0), p. 37; © Adam Hart-Davis/Science Source, p. 38; © Science Source, p. 42; © iStockphoto.com/Cesare Ferarri (light burst).

Front cover: © iStockphoto.com/pixel1962.